Why me?

Pete Guppy

SURVIVAL

RISING ★ STARS

in association with

nasen
Helping Everyone Achieve

NASEN House, 4/5 Amber Business Village, Amber Close, Amington,
Tamworth, Staffordshire B77 4RP

Rising Stars UK Ltd.
22 Grafton Street, London W1S 4EX
www.risingstars-uk.com

Published 2009

Cover design: Roger Warham
Cover image: Photofusion Picture Library/Alamy
Text design and typesetting: Roger Warham
Publisher: Gill Budgell
Editorial consultant: Lorraine Petersen

British Library Cataloguing in Publication Data.

A CIP record for this book is available from the British Library.

ISBN: 978-1-84680-603-2

Printed in the UK by CPI Bookmarque, Croydon, CR0 4TD

Hi, Bugs. Meet me outside the main gates after school. Don't be late. Butch.

RISING STARS

SURVIVAL

Chapter 1

"They put your head down the toilet. Then they flush it," his sister said in his ear. Words turned to pictures in Wayne's head.

"Then they hold your head down so you can't breathe," she added.

More pictures rushed into his mind and a frightened look came onto his face. His mum saw the look.

"What are you saying to Wayne?" she asked.

"Nothing," said his sister.

"I hope you're not saying anything about his new school. You know he's a bit nervous about his first day," said his mum. She came over to him and said, "You just remember what I told you. Get there on time, keep your head down, and work hard."

"Oh, they'll keep his head down," said his sister, and she laughed so much she couldn't put on her lip-gloss.

"What's so funny?" asked his mum.

"It's nothing. She's being stupid," said Wayne. He picked up his bag and went to the door.

His sister called out, "Have a nice day at the big boys' school. Don't keep your head down too long."

Wayne slammed the door on her laugh.

But her words stayed with him.

"It can't be true," he said to himself. But she had said it so often he felt it must be.

His walk to school got slower, and slower. Then he stopped and looked at himself in a shop window. Looking back was a skinny lad, lost inside a jacket that was too big for him.

Two front teeth stuck out over a bottom lip. And the new haircut didn't make him look hard at all.

"What chance have I got if they grab me? They could pick me up and use me as a bog brush," he said to himself.

With a feeling of doom he went on his way, eyes down and feet dragging along the pavement. Everything about him said, "Victim. Come and pick on me."

So they did.

Three older boys and two girls spotted him as he reached the school gates.

"I think we've got a new boy," shouted one of the lads.

"I like your jacket. How many people can you get in it?" shouted one of the girls.

"Did your mummy tell you you'd grow into it? Well you might in another ten years," yelled the other girl.

Then they spotted his two front teeth.

"Maybe it's not a boy at all. With teeth like that it could be a rabbit," said the first lad.

"I know who it is. It's Bugs Bunny," said one of the girls. They all laughed.

"What's up, Doc? What's up, Doc?" they began shouting, as they pretended to eat carrots.

Wayne kept his head down and walked on.

"Welcome to the school, Bugs. See you in the toilets," they shouted.

That did it!

Wayne's slow walk turned into a fast zigzag as he dashed onto the playground.

The gang saw him run, and gave a cheer. Showing fear was just what they wanted to see. It fed their hunger for power.

Wayne's mad dash took him round the back of the sports hall. He hid there until the bell went.

The welcoming party at the gate had upset him. He'd wanted to make friends, but now he didn't know who to trust or who to talk to.

That's how two bad habits began; keeping out of sight at break times, and only nodding to teachers when they spoke to him in class.

By the end of his first day in secondary school he'd kept his eyes down and his mouth shut.

And he'd kept well away from the toilets.

That's why he was the first one out of the gates when the bell rang. Rushing home, he rammed his key in the lock and dashed upstairs to the toilet. He was just in time.

"So, how was your first day?" asked his mum, as she came in from work.

"Fine. No problems," said Wayne.

"Did you enjoy your first day?" his dad asked, when he'd locked up his shop.

"Fine. No problems," said Wayne.

"Did you go to the toilets?" asked his sister.

"Yes. No problems," hissed Wayne.

With those three lies, Wayne was making another mistake. He wasn't telling anyone about his fears. He was keeping them all to himself.

The next morning, he had a long face at breakfast. He picked at his food and didn't pick a fight with his sister.

"Are you feeling ok?" asked Mum.

"Yes, thanks," lied Wayne.

"Do you want a lift to school?" she asked.

"No, thanks," said Wayne.

"Are you sure?" she asked again.

"Yes," Wayne nodded.

"Leave him alone. He wants to go on his own," said his dad, from behind his newspaper.

"But it's not easy for him. He doesn't know anyone there. He missed the first week of term because we've been moving closer to the shop," his mum said.

"I'm OK. I can handle it," said Wayne crossly.

But as he walked to school he couldn't think of a plan. They were older and bigger, and he was frightened of them. He just hoped and prayed they would leave him alone.

Chapter 2

"Hi, Bugs. Didn't see you in the toilets, yesterday. Don't rabbits need a dump?"

Wayne rushed past the waiting gang of five.

"That's right. Hop along, Bugs Bunny."

With his head down, Wayne slunk to the far end of the playground. He stood watching the rest of the kids around him.

They were chatting and laughing as if they had known each other forever. It all seemed like one big party. But he was on the outside, looking in. It just seemed easier to stay there.

For the rest of the week his hand stayed down in class. He hid himself away at break times and lunch. And he stayed well away from the toilets. Until Friday!

On Friday, there was a smell in the room, Wayne put his hand up.

"I need the toilet, Miss," he said to his teacher.

"Can't it wait until break?" she asked.

Wayne's white face and bent body gave the answer. He tried running to the toilet but all he could do was a crab-like shuffle with his legs together.

He was still on the seat when the bell rang for break. Into the toilet came the Smoking Club.

Wayne slid the bolt on the door and started praying.

"Bloody hell. Who's died in here?" gasped a smoker. "It smells worse than my old man after a curry," said another.

"Let's get a fag going, fast," said a voice that Wayne knew.

Smoke began to drift across the toilets.

"That's better," said a smoker, blowing out a lungful of smoke.

"I wonder what dirty little git left that stink behind?"

Then someone spotted that one of the toilet doors was closed.

"Maybe they haven't left yet. Maybe that dirty little git is still with us," said another voice.

Wayne stopped breathing. Then the door in front of him shook as someone kicked it.

"I think Stinker is still at home, boys," said a smoker, gleefully. "I wonder who it is?"

Suddenly, a face looked under the door and yelled out, "It's Bugs! It's Bugs Bunny with his pants down!"

The smokers went wild. There was shouting, clapping, cheering and hammering on doors. Hands reached in trying to get him.

Wayne pulled up his trousers and sat wide-eyed with fear. There was nowhere to go, nowhere to hide.

"Are you coming out, or are we coming in?" one of them yelled.

"Because one way or another, it's time to flush the rabbit."

Like a football crowd, the rest of the smokers took up the chant.

"Flush the rabbit, flush the rabbit, flush the rabbit."

Wayne's eyes filled with tears. It wasn't fair. He hadn't done anything to these kids. Why were they picking on him?

The noise in the toilets got even louder as one of the smokers started to climb over the door.

"Flush the rabbit, flush the rabbit."

Wayne knew his sister's words were about to come true.

Suddenly, a louder voice yelled out above the din.

"OUT! The lot of you. And I'm not just talking about your fags."

It was Mr Jeffries, the maths teacher. He had heard the noise on his way to playground duty.

"I said OUT! Before I put the lot of you in detention. You know smoking isn't allowed."

Everything happened fast. The shouting and hammering stopped. Hands and faces vanished from Wayne's sight. Fags were put out. Soon, the only thing left of the Smoking Club was their smoke.

As soon as they had all gone, Mr Jeffries called over the door to Wayne.

"Are you all right in there?" he asked.

"I'm not on top of the world, sir," said Wayne.

Mr Jeffries laughed until he choked. When he got his breath back he said, "Well, you can come out now. You're safe."

Wayne sorted himself out and opened the door.

"So, what was that all about?" asked Mr Jeffries.

"Nothing, sir," said Wayne. But his face told a different story.

"*They* didn't seem to think it was nothing. Have you been borrowing fags and not paying them back?" asked Mr Jeffries.

Wayne shook his head. "I don't smoke, sir."

"Good for you. It's a bad habit," he said.

"So why were they making so much noise? You don't often hear them. You just smell their smoke," said Mr Jeffries.

"It was just a bit of fun, sir," said Wayne.

Mr Jeffries nodded, "I haven't seen you around school before."

"I only started this week, sir," said Wayne.

"What's your name?" asked Mr Jeffries.

"Wayne Peters, sir."

"Are you settling in, OK?" he asked.

"Yes, sir," said Wayne.

Mr Jeffries took a long look at him.

"Are you being picked on?" he asked.

"No," said Wayne, hoping his face didn't show the lie.

"Well, if you say you're ok, I'll be off," he said.

Wayne relaxed. The questions were over.

"Just as long as it's not that old story about having your head put down the toilet," said Mr Jeffries.

"That's just a story to frighten new boys. Now, off you go."

Wayne was still shaken up but he began to smile. His head wasn't going down the toilet and he was going to have fun killing his sister at the weekend!

Chapter 3

It was a record. Wayne was up, washed, dressed and downstairs before his mum's first shout.

Nicking his dad's toast and picking up his school bag, he was out of the house before anyone could stop him.

"Wow. That's a first. I didn't think he was enjoying his new school," said his mum.

"I told you he'd work things out. You worry too much," his dad said.

Getting up early was all part of Wayne's plan for his second week at school. He was going to get there before the gang met at the gates. Then he was going to hide until lessons started.

Having a plan made him feel better and he began looking around as he walked the early morning streets. There was plenty to see and hear.

Postmen rattled letter boxes and milkmen clinked bottles. Vans flashed their hazard lights as they parked on double yellow lines. A biker on the pavement just missed a man as he left the shop reading his paper.

Two dogs being taken for a walk stopped to sniff each other. The dogs owners had small plastic bags in their hands.

"It must be good being a dog and having someone walk behind you, cleaning up your mess. I bet they don't even do that for the Queen," Wayne said to himself.

He smiled as a man on a bike shouted rude words at a car driver who had almost run him down.

"Why don't you look where you're _____ well going, you _____ fool!" Wayne's smile turned to shock when he saw the face under the helmet. It was Mr Jeffries.

"Morning, Mr Jeffries," Wayne called out. Mr Jeffries pretended not to hear and rode off with a red face under a red helmet.

Then along the pavement came another red face. This one was puffing and panting as the runner went past.

Without thinking, Wayne began running alongside him.

"Are you a footballer?" he asked.

"No, I'm not," shouted the man. Wayne didn't take the hint.

"Are you training for a Marathon?"

"No," said the man, sweat dripping off him.

"You're not going very fast," said Wayne.

Red-face stopped running and jogged on the spot. He fixed his eyes on Wayne.

A left jab just missed Wayne's right ear. Then a right fist flew past his left ear. Wayne took a step back.

"I'm a boxer, lad. If you think it's easy, try running five miles every morning. Then hit a punch bag for 30 minutes, skip for 30 minutes, and finish off with boxing for an hour."

Wayne took the hint, and stayed rooted to the spot as the boxer jogged off down a side street.

Then he looked at his watch and ran the rest of the way to school.

Five minutes later, he was standing on an empty playground. His plan was working.

He spent the next 45 minutes by a wall next to the car park, watching the teachers drive in. Most of the cars were boring but one or two were cool.

The French teacher got out of a soft-top sports car and said, "Bonjour," to the boys standing by her car.

An old looking teacher struggled out of his flashy red car.

"You're too old for that car," thought Wayne. Then in zoomed a great looking motorbike. Under the black leathers and black helmet was one of the young P.E. teachers.

He walked into school with a few giggling girls by his side.

"Nice one," thought Wayne. "That's better than old Jeffries on his push bike."

Twenty minutes later, Wayne was in his first lesson of the day.

Getting to school early had kept him away from the gang, and he felt safer now he was in class. He was pleased with himself, and he had the beginnings of a smile on his face.

He turned in his chair to take a book out of his bag. But when he turned back his warm glow became a cold chill. On his desk was a carrot with teeth marks in it.

He looked around to see who had put it there, but he couldn't tell. Everyone looked as if they were working. Wayne stuffed the carrot in his bag and got on with the lesson.

His smile had gone. He knew what was going on. It was the gang telling him that there was nowhere to hide. That they could always get to him. And they did.

They found his hiding places around the school and poked fun at him.

They slapped him too hard on the back, pretending to be friends.

They kicked their ball at him as he walked across the playground.

They bumped into him when he was carrying a drink. And they chased him home, shouting, "_____ off home, rabbit teeth. We'll get you tomorrow. And don't listen to Jeffries. Your head is still going down the toilet."

He also became a target in the classroom.

When books were being handed out, his was thrown at him. Rolled up paper hit him on the back of the head. A leg tripped him up. His books were knocked off his desk. Things went missing from his bag.

They were all small things, not easy for the teachers to spot. But as the weeks went by, they added up in Wayne's mind.

He didn't know why he was being picked on. He hadn't hurt anyone.

But as no one else in his class was being bullied, he began blaming himself.

It must all be his fault. He felt ashamed of himself.

But he didn't want to make things worse by telling anyone about it. So he kept it to himself, hoping it would go away.

It didn't.

The more he hid from them, the more they came after him.

The jokes became threats. The tripping became pushing. The pen stealing became hair pulling.

Wayne didn't know what to do, so he did nothing.

He didn't trust anyone in class, and he was ratty with everyone at home. He was not eating, not sleeping and jumpy. Getting out of bed and going to school each day got more and more difficult.

He felt the bullying would never stop.

Chapter 4

The gang were waiting for him outside school. Two of them pinned him against a wall. The rest stood round him.

"We seem to have the rabbit in a trap," said one.

"What shall we do with him?" asked another. The biggest lad took something out of his pocket.

"Maybe it's time to put him out of his misery," he said and he slid his finger across his throat as he spoke.

Wayne struggled, but he couldn't get free.

"As we didn't get to flush the rabbit. I think it's time to skin him," said the big lad.

"Skin the rabbit," hissed the gang.

Wayne's legs went weak and he shut his eyes. He felt something hard and cold on his cheek.

"My name is Butcher. But you can call me Butch," said the lad.

A thought flashed into Wayne's head. They were going to kill him.

"Would you like this nightmare to end? Would you like to have some friends?" asked Butch.

Wayne nodded slowly, keeping his eyes shut.

"I can make that happen," said Butch.

Wayne stood still, hardly breathing.

"You see, you have to be a friend to have a friend. Are you a friend of mine?" asked Butch.

Something pressed harder into Wayne's cheek.

"Yes," said Wayne, tears running down his face.

"Friends help each other, don't they?" asked Butch.

"Yes," said Wayne.

"So, you are going to help me by getting me some fags, now and then," said Butch.

Butch's hand moved down onto Wayne's neck.

"You can get them from your dad's shop, can't you?" asked Butch.

Wayne kept his eyes and mouth shut. But his brain was working overtime.

So that was it. If he wanted an easy time at school, he had to steal from his dad!

Butch pressed harder and Wayne found himself saying, "Yes."

"Good. Now open your eyes, Bugs Bunny. Meet your new friends," said Butch.

Wayne opened his eyes. The gang were smiling at him and Butch patted Wayne on top of his head.

"Now hop along home, little rabbit. Get me a pack of twenty by Friday. Your dad won't miss one pack of fags."

Then they were gone, chatting and laughing as they went off up the road.

Wayne dried his eyes and tried to stop shaking. Maybe things were going to get better.

All he had to do was take a few fags from his dad's shop and the bullying would stop.

He began planning. It wouldn't really be stealing because he'd pay for the fags with his pocket money. He wouldn't need to do it often.

Wayne began to smile. Life was going to get better.

At first, his plan went well. He took the fags and put the money in the till when his dad was in the stockroom. Then he handed them to Butch outside the school gates.

Butch called off his troops. The bullying stopped and Wayne was happy. He'd found an answer to his problem. Butch was also happy. He'd got Wayne doing just what he wanted.

Two weeks later, Butch came asking for another pack of twenty.

Then he started asking for a pack a week. All of Wayne's pocket money was now spent on keeping Butch happy.

Wayne felt it was worth it. It was great not being picked on.

But Butch liked the feeling of power. Soon he was asking for two packets of fags a week.

"I haven't got the money," pleaded Wayne.

"That's your problem, Bugs. Get them to me by next Monday, or it all starts again," said Butch.

Wayne had three days to sort something out. He had to get some cash.

He tried to get a job as a paper boy but couldn't. He tried to borrow money from his sister.

"Push off. You never pay me back," she said.

He asked his dad for two weeks pocket money.

"Why do you need the money?" he asked.

Wayne shrugged. "I just do," he said.

"Well, you need to learn the value of money. You'll have to wait," said his dad.

Wayne couldn't wait. He needed Butch's fags and he needed them quickly. He knew the value of money. It stopped him being bullied.

Chapter 5

Time was running out for Wayne. It was
Monday morning and he still hadn't got
the fags.

He hung around his dad's shop, waiting for
him to nip out for his morning coffee. As
soon as his dad left, Wayne went in.

"Morning, Janet. It's only me. I've come to
change a £10 note," he said.

Janet was stacking shelves at the back of the shop. She had worked for his dad for years.

"Hi, Wayne," she shouted.

Wayne opened the till and put in the money for one pack of twenty. Then he looked across at Janet. She had her back to him. He turned quickly and grabbed two packs off the shelf. He put them in his pocket and shut the till.

"See you, Janet," he said, as he dashed out of the shop. Janet stood watching him as he jogged up the road to school.

It wasn't stealing, Wayne told himself. He wasn't *stealing* fags from his dad. He was *borrowing* them until he could pay for them. The borrowing went on for the next few weeks.

It was risky and deep down he knew it was wrong. But it was helping his school life run smoothly.

Then a note was passed to him in class when the teacher wasn't looking.

Hi, Bugs. Meet me outside the main gates after school. Don't be late. Butch.

Wayne didn't want a meeting with Butch, so he left by the back way. He ran smack into the gang!

"You weren't trying to stay away from me, were you?" asked Butch.

"No," said Wayne, trying to back away from them, but there was a wall in his way.

"Good. Because now I want three packs of twenty every week, and a bottle of vodka. I've got to keep my troops happy," said Butch.

Wayne stood open-mouthed.

"I can't get all that," he said.

"Yes you can. It will all fit in your jacket pocket," said Butch.

"I won't do it," said Wayne.

Butch sneered at him.

"I think you will, Bugs. Or I'll make your life hell," he said.

The gang left Wayne with a sinking feeling in his belly. He was paying a high price for an easy life at school.

Over the next three weeks, Wayne got the fags and vodka from behind the counter in his dad's shop.

Then he came unstuck.

His dad had just nipped out, leaving Janet in the shop. Wayne went in.

"Hi, Janet," he said.

"Hi, Wayne. Watch the shop for me, would you? I'm just going into the stockroom," she said.

Wayne was behind the counter faster than you could blink. But he couldn't find any vodka. He gave up looking and reached up for the fags. He put two packs in his pocket. He was taking a third pack off the shelf, when he heard a voice behind him,

"I think that should go back on the shelf, Wayne."

Wayne turned to see Janet coming out of the stockroom. He'd taken too long looking for the vodka. He looked at the packet of fags in his hand, and had a brainwave.

"I'm buying them for my mates at school. Look, I've got the money," he said.

He took out his money and put it in the till.

"Your dad wouldn't like it," said Janet. Wayne acted quickly.

"Then don't tell him," he said.

He was out of the shop in a flash.

"I've got away with it. She didn't see me take the other two packs and I don't think she'll tell Dad," he said to himself.

He was right. Janet didn't say a word to his dad. She had always liked Wayne and didn't want to get him into trouble. But she didn't know about all the fags and vodka that had been going missing.
His dad did!

He checked his stock every week, and it was puzzling him.

Shoplifting was a problem for every shopkeeper. But these things were always kept behind the counter and only he, his family and Janet ever went behind there.

He had a feeling he knew who was stealing from him. If he was right, she would have to go.

Chapter 6

The house shook as Wayne's dad slammed the door on his way out.

"What's up with him?" asked Wayne.

"Problems in the shop. Things have been going missing over the last two months," said his mum.

Wayne's heart missed a beat.

"What things?" he asked.

"Vodka and cigarettes. He thinks Janet has been taking them. He's very angry. He's thinking of sacking her," she said.

Wayne's legs went weak and he sat down.

"But he hasn't got... I mean, has he got proof that it's Janet?" he asked.

His mum looked at him.

"No. But who else could it be?" she asked. Her question hung in the air.

Wayne shrugged but didn't look at his mum.

"Dunno. Maybe it's shoplifters," he said.

"But it's only us, and Janet, who go behind the counter," said Mum.

Wayne went pale. His mum went on, "Anyway, your dad says that if one more packet of cigarettes goes missing, he will talk to Janet about it."

Wayne felt sick.

"Are you all right?" asked his mum.

"Yes, I'm just not hungry," he lied.

Wayne got out of the house as fast as he could. He walked to school, trying not to panic. If he took one more pack of fags, Janet could get the sack. If he didn't get fags and vodka, he'd get picked on again. But, if he kept stealing from the shop, his dad would soon know it was him.

Wayne didn't know what to do.

He didn't want to get Janet mixed up in this. She had always been kind to him. And she needed the job. She was bringing up two children on her own.

Wayne's day had started badly. Then he got another note from Butch. It said,

Same time. Same place.
Don't be late.

Wayne dragged himself to the meeting place.

"Don't look so sad, Bugs Bunny. I've got some good news for you," said Butch.

For a split second, Wayne thought they were going to leave him alone. Then he saw the look on Butch's face.

"It's nearly Christmas, and we'd like you to come to our party. But you'll need to bring three packs of fags and a *big* bottle of vodka," said Butch.

The gang fell around laughing.

"I can't get any more," said Wayne.

The laughing stopped.

"I hope you're joking, little rabbit," said Butch.

"My dad knows someone is stealing stuff. He thinks it's the lady who works for him. She might get the sack," said Wayne.

Butch said, "But he doesn't know it's you. So who cares if she gets the sack? Silly old cow."

There was fear in Wayne's face. But there was anger as well.

He was angry with himself for being so helpless and he was angry with Butch for talking about Janet like that.

The anger and fear boiled up inside him and he made a run for it!

The gang were slow to move. Wayne was skinny, but he was fast.

"You can run, but you can't hide. You might as well stop right now," yelled Butch.

Wayne's legs weren't stopping. They took him down the road, round the corner, up the main street, and into a side street.

His legs were working well, but his brain wasn't.

It was a dead end!

Wayne hid in a doorway, trying to get his brain into gear. Did he have time to get back to the main street?

A look up the side street gave him the answer. Two of the gang were coming down it, checking the doorways.

Wayne had nowhere to hide.

He was trapped.

He turned and looked at the door behind him. He could see light shining under it.

Wayne pushed and pulled the handle, but the door was locked.

Butch and the gang flashed into his mind and he began to panic.

He tried the door again. But it was no good. All he could do now was make a run for it.

He was going to go on the count of three. But as he got to two, the door opened behind him.

Wayne spun round and a voice said,

"Well, if it isn't my running friend."

It was the boxer he had seen out training.

"You were rattling that door good and hard. Do you want to have a go at boxing then? Good lad. Come in and I'll show you around," he said.

Wayne stepped into the light. The door closed behind him, shutting out his fears.

Chapter 7

The boxing club was filled with the sounds of training. Fists thudded into punch bags. Feet pounded the wooden floor. Bar bells clanked. A drumming sound came from the punching of a speedball.

Grunts and groans came from boxers doing pull-ups, press-ups and sit-ups.

A man, who was shadow-boxing, made short, sharp, snorting sounds as he jabbed and punched thin air. Above all these sounds, a voice shouted, "Don't just stand there. Jab and move, jab and move."

A white-haired man was watching two young boxers in the ring. They didn't look much older than Wayne.

"Stop hanging on to each other. You're boxing, not dancing," he told them.

As he watched the boxers, Wayne began to daydream. Wouldn't it be great to be good at fighting? He could take on the whole gang. He could get Butch on the floor and hit him, and kick him and...

"I said, are you thinking of joining the club?" asked the boxer, who was showing Wayne round. Wayne snapped out of his daydream, and nodded his head.

"You're not talking as much as the last time we met," said the boxer.

Wayne shook his head, and then asked, "Can I start now?"

"What's all the rush?" asked the boxer.

Wayne just looked at the floor. But there was something in his look that made the boxer stop and think.

"Well, I've finished my training for today. I could give you a bit of a fitness test," he said.

Wayne nodded and almost smiled.

"I'll go and get you some spare kit. We've always got some around." He came back with a T-shirt and shorts.

"Put these on. You can leave your shoes on. But tie the laces, don't just tuck them down the sides," he said.

When Wayne was ready, the boxer said,

"My name's Don. What's yours?" Wayne told him and they shook hands.

"OK. Let's see what you can do," said Don.

Wayne did six sit-ups, but then got cramp. He did three press-ups, but then his arms couldn't get his nose off the floor. He lay there smelling the stink of past boxers.

He tried doing a pull-up but couldn't get his chin above the bar. He pulled and strained until his eyes nearly popped out. Then he hung there like a sleeping bat.

Don helped him down from the bar.

"Getting you fit could take time," he said.

"I haven't got much time," muttered Wayne.

"Pardon?" said Don.

"Nothing," said Wayne.

Don took Wayne over to watch a boxer speed skipping. The rope moved so fast it was just a blur. The boxer's hands and feet worked as one, making it look easy.

Don gave a rope to Wayne. But he trod on it, tripped over it, and got tangled up in it.

"It takes practice," smiled Don.

"How much?" asked Wayne.

"Depends how hard you work," said Don.

"Can I come here every day?" asked Wayne.

"That's not up to me. That's up to the coach. He's over there with the punch pads," said Don.

Wayne looked across at the white-haired man who had been with the two boxers in the ring. He had big pads on his hands, which he was holding up for a young boxer to hit.

The boxer slammed his left fist into the coach's left hand. Then the right fist came across, hitting the right-hand pad.

Left, slam. Right, slam. Left, slam. Right, slam. Wayne began to smile. This was more like it.

"Hit the dot," said the coach.

"What does he mean?" asked Wayne.

"The pads have got a dot in the middle of them. It helps the boxer focus on what to hit," said Don.

Wayne knew what he wanted to hit.

"How long does it take to learn how to punch?" he asked.

Don shrugged, "It takes as long as it takes."

Wayne looked puzzled.

"You've got to learn the right footwork. You've got to get the timing right. You've got to learn when to punch, and how to take a punch. Boxing isn't just about hitting people," said Don.

It wasn't the answer Wayne wanted to hear.

"Can I have a go at hitting the pads?" he asked.

"That's up to the coach. You sit down and wait for him. I'm off for a shower," said Don.

Wayne watched as he waited. He'd expected all boxers to be big and powerful looking. But they weren't.

Some were, but others were as skinny as he was. They still looked good and it gave Wayne hope. He drifted into his daydream again.

"So you want to be a boxer, do you?"

Wayne woke from his daydream to find the coach by his side. He was a short, stocky man with a face that had taken some punches in its time. His nose was bent and battered and he had scars around his eyes. His short, white hair didn't hide his large, flat ears.

This man knew about fighting.

"Don't worry, you won't end up looking like me. Not if you listen," he said.

Wayne was lost for words.

"Do you still want to join?" asked the coach.

Wayne nodded, trying to drag his eyes away from the crooked and mangled nose.

"OK, if you come back tomorrow, I'll have a look at you," said the coach. Wayne nodded, spotting a tattoo of an eagle on his strong arm.

"Tell your parents and bring some kit. Now I'll show you out," said the coach.

Out in the side street, Wayne checked to see if the gang were waiting for him.

Then he shadow-boxed his way home in the dark.

Chapter 8

Bunking off school was the only way he could stay away from the gang. But telling his mum he was ill wouldn't work.

So for the last three days of term, Wayne put his kit and some Mars bars in his bag, and left the house at the normal time.

He spent the first day in the park and was back at the boxing club before the end of school.

The coach opened the door. "You're keen. Shouldn't you still be at school?" he asked.

"They've let us out early because it's the last week of term," lied Wayne.

"OK, come in and get your kit on," he said.

Wayne got changed in a scruffy old room, lit by a single bulb that gave a yellowish light. The smell of sweat was everywhere. He tied the laces of his trainers and went out into the training room.

The coach said, "First of all, we do a warm-up. We'll jog, run and sprint on the spot."

They started slowly but Wayne's arms and legs were soon pumping like mad. He was gasping for air when they stopped.

"Now I want to watch you do the exercises you did with Don. Press-ups first," said the coach.

Wayne got down on the floor.

"Do the exercises slowly. It's not how many you do, it's how well you do them," he said.

Wayne did three, his nose going down to the floor each time.

"Now the sit-ups. Don't rush them," he said. Wayne did five good ones.

Then it was leg stretches and skipping.

"You can do these exercises at home. But don't do more than I tell you," said the coach.

"Can I have a go at hitting the pads?" asked Wayne.

"No. You need to be fitter and stronger before you hit anything. You also need to know about footwork and how to make a fist," he said.

Wayne looked downcast. He didn't want to know all that. He just wanted to know how to punch someone's lights out.

The coach saw the look.

"I'll do a deal with you. It'll be Christmas in ten days' time. If you can show me you've worked hard at your exercises, I'll let you have a go at hitting the pads on Christmas Eve," he said.

Wayne smiled.

"Can I come to the club every day?" he asked.

"If you do, keep your eyes open. Look at the way the boxers train and spar. Now, off you go and get a shower. I've got to help the boxers who are coming in from work," said the coach.

Wayne had a shower and dried himself on a grubby-looking towel. Then he set off for home.

"You're late home from school, again," said his mum, when he walked in the house.

"I've been hanging out with some new mates," he said.

Wayne worked hard for the next ten days. He missed the last three days of school but he learnt a lot from watching the boxers train. He began doing his exercises at home as well.

"I see you've started running every day," his mum said.

"Yes," said Wayne.

"Is this fitness bug going to last long?" she asked.

But all his hard work paid off. On the afternoon of Christmas Eve, Wayne showed the coach how much better he was at the exercises.

"Good lad. That's much better," he said.

The coach took hold of Wayne's left hand. "Now, make a fist," he said. Wayne closed his fingers to make a fist.

"Keep it tight and don't let your thumb stick out. Keep the back of your hand flat with the rest of your arm," he said.

"Don't let your fist stick up or you could crack a bone when you punch."

The coach put training gloves on Wayne's hands and big pads on his own.

"Come on, then. You've seen the other boxers do it. Hit the pads," said the coach.

Wayne began with a good fast left jab. Then he crossed with a right.

"Not bad. Do it again," said the coach.

Wayne did it again. Left, right. Left, right.

"Keep your wrist level with the rest of your arm. Go again," said the coach.

Wayne jabbed and punched himself to a standstill. He stood with his hands hanging down, too heavy to lift.

"You did well. You've got good fast hands. You'd score points in a contest with those punches," said the coach.

It wasn't points Wayne was thinking of.

"Can I have a go on the big punch bag?" he asked.

"OK. But think of your fists as balls of rock and punch with your knuckles," said the coach.

He wiped some sweat off Wayne's forehead and drew a face on the punch bag.

"Punch at the face," he said.

Wayne saw Butch's face and he gave the bag a hell of a crack with his right hand.

The bag didn't move, but Wayne did as his arm crumpled into it.

"No more punching, today," said the coach, as he pulled the gloves off Wayne.

"When can I get into the ring and learn how to fight?" asked Wayne.

"You mean, when can you learn how to box?" said the coach. "If you keep doing well with your exercises and hitting the pads, I'll put you in the ring in a week's time."

That was just before school started again. This was better than a Christmas present.

"When does the club open after Christmas?" asked Wayne.

"The day after Boxing Day," said the coach.

"So you don't box on Boxing Day. Funny that," smiled Wayne, as he went off for a shower.

Chapter 9

His training gloves came a long way up his arms and felt like big cotton-wool balls.

His head guard kept slipping down over his eyes. His gum shield fitted badly in his mouth. But Wayne was in the ring and ready to box.

The coach was keeping to his word, and Wayne had kept at his training. He had even gone running on Christmas Day.

The coach said to Wayne, "I want to see good footwork and sharp punching." Then he said to the other boxer, "Take it easy with Wayne. It's his first time. OK. Touch gloves and come out fighting," said the coach.

The two boxers touched gloves.

Then Wayne forgot everything he had been told. He went forward, his arms like a windmill in a gale. He walked straight into a left jab.

Bells rang in his head, his legs went weak and his backside hit the floor.

"Don't rush at him. Step and punch," said the coach.

Wayne got to his feet. They touched gloves.

Wayne threw two wild, looping punches and walked into another jab. Down he went again.

He didn't think it was going to hurt like this.

"Come on. A smack in the face isn't going to kill you. It's only pain," said the coach.

Wayne didn't agree.

He got to his feet, wiping tears away with his gloves. He was getting angry. He wanted to punch, not be punched. He ran and swung a right-hander. The boxer stepped to one side and jabbed Wayne's head.

Wayne was getting mad.

The gang had picked on him and laughed at him. He'd been bullied and chased. He'd felt fear, anger and shame. Now his head was being punched.

It was too much and he lost it.

Wayne ran at the boxer, kicking and punching as he went.

"Bullies. I hate bullies. I want to kill them all," he screamed, as his gum shield shot out.

The boxer put his head down behind his gloves and covered up. He just let the storm of punches rain down on him.

As Wayne aimed another kick, strong hands picked him up and took him to the other side of the ring.

"He's not bullying you," said the coach.

"I mean the ones at school," shouted Wayne.

The coach let go of Wayne's arms.

"So that's it. That's why you've been coming here. I think it's time you told me all about it," he said.

Wayne hadn't spoken to anyone about being bullied. He'd kept it all bottled up inside. Now, it was like a dam bursting as he told the coach everything.

When the tears and talking stopped, the coach took the gloves and head guard off Wayne. Then he said, "It's useful if you can throw a punch, Wayne. But fighting isn't the answer. I know. I've tried. By the time I was twenty-five, I'd spent six years in jail. All because I couldn't walk away from a fight."

"But I want the bullying to stop," said Wayne.

"So why didn't you tell someone about it?" asked the coach.

"I thought it would make it worse," said Wayne.

"You need to tell a teacher you trust. Then tell your parents," Coach replied.

Wayne didn't look happy.

The coach went on, "You didn't ask to be bullied, Wayne. But your teachers need to know what's going on. You may not be the only one."

Wayne nodded.

"Now let's see what you can do to help yourself. First of all, you've got to stop walking like a victim.

You need to walk with your head up and your shoulders back. Stop looking afraid. Look people in the eye," the coach said.

Wayne nodded, and stood taller.

"What do you say when the gang call you names?" asked the coach.

"Nothing," said Wayne.

"Well you need to make a list of things to say. Try and make them funny," said the coach.

Wayne nodded, and started to think.

"And I want you back here tomorrow. You're going back in the ring," he said.

Wayne nodded, and smiled.

Then the coach said, "But I won't have you acting like a thug. Not in the ring or out on the street. If you act badly, it reflects badly on me and on the club. I won't have that. Do you understand me?" he asked.

"Yes, Coach," said Wayne.

"Now, before you have a shower, go and say sorry to Gary. He's the lad you tried to kill in the ring," said the coach.

Wayne did as he was told. Then he had a shower, and went home to more cold turkey and chips.

Chapter 10

The next day, Wayne was back in the ring.
He was keeping his fists up, his chin down
and his temper in check. He was on his
toes, stepping and punching, jabbing and
moving. This time he didn't rush in.

He watched and waited, looking for
openings, watching for punches. It gave him
that split second to move.

Some punches still hit him but they didn't hurt as much. Wayne was learning how to box.

The two boxers touched gloves at the end of the workout.

"Much better. You moved well and used your fast hands. Keep listening to me and I'll make a boxer out of you, yet," said the coach.

A smile started somewhere deep inside, and slowly made its way onto Wayne's face. He was starting to feel good about himself again.

"When do you go back to school?" asked the coach.

"Monday," said Wayne.

"Do you know which teacher you're going to speak to?" he asked.

"Yes," said Wayne, his smile fading.

"And don't forget to tell your parents," he said.

"No," said Wayne, looking unhappy.

"Get it over with. Then come and see me on Monday after school. You can tell me what's been said."

"Yes Coach," sighed Wayne.

But it was the gang who wanted the last word.

It was Sunday, and Wayne was on a training run. He was thinking what it would be like to win a gold medal. Then he turned a corner and ran straight into the gang.

"Well, what have we got here?" sneered Butch. "Bugs Bunny in his boxer shorts, with skinny little legs. If I had legs like yours, I'd keep them covered up."

For the very first time, Wayne looked him straight in the eye. "And if I had a brain like yours, I'd keep it in a matchbox," he said.

Butch looked shocked. He took a step forward.

Wayne stood his ground, fists up, and ready.

Butch was older and bigger, but he didn't take another step.

"You couldn't punch your way out of a paper bag," said Butch.

"Come a bit closer and find out," said Wayne. Butch sneered, but there was a flicker of fear in his face. Wayne saw it.

"I could beat you with one hand tied behind my back," said Butch.

"What will you be doing with the other one? Scratching your bum with it?" asked Wayne.

Some of the gang laughed. Butch didn't like it. He was lost for words.

One of the girls said, "I could knock you over with one good slap."

"I'll bet you could, you _____. Why don't you try then?" said Wayne.

The girl didn't move.

Butch found his voice.

"You're still going to steal for me. Or we'll make your life hell."

"I'm not stealing for you, or for your stupid mates EVER again," said Wayne.

It was an insult too far. One of the gang ran at him and threw a punch.

Wayne's feet moved quickly, but his eyes never left the target. As the bully came past, Wayne shot out a fist. A good solid punch smacked into his nose. He yelped in pain and a shocked look came onto his face. Then he ran at Wayne, again.

Same footwork. Same punch. Same nose. But the yelp was louder, and there was blood this time.

As the bully put a hand up to his face, Wayne moved in and hit him hard in the belly.

Like his coach had said, "If you're going to hit, hit hard."

Then he stepped back. He was a boxer, not a thug.

The punch had knocked the wind and fight out of the bully. It made the others stop and think too. But then they all moved towards him.

"You think you can take us all on, don't you?" shouted one of the girls.

"I don't have to. I'm not staying quiet any more. You lot are finished. It's over," said Wayne.

It took a few seconds for his words to sink in. Butch could see that Wayne meant it.

"Come on. He's not worth it. Let's leave Bugs Bunny to his stupid boxing," said Butch.

And off the gang went, four swaggering and one struggling.

Wayne walked away on shaky legs.

Was that it? Was it all over? Or would they try and pick on him, again.

If they did, he was ready for them. He wasn't going to back off, ever again. He didn't feel alone any more. There was the club, his coach, his teachers and parents.

Wayne began jogging on stronger legs. He couldn't wait to tell his coach all about it.

But maybe he'd wait before telling Mr Jeffries and his parents . . .

Sometimes, you just have to box clever.

Look out for other exciting stories in the
Survival series:

Jet Scream
Stormy Waters
The Gambling Habit
Runaway
The Boss
Fireproof
Why Me?
Flirting with Danger

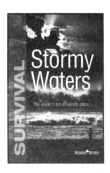
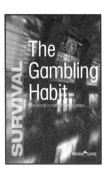

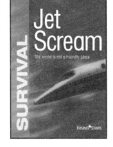
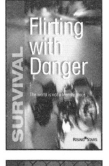

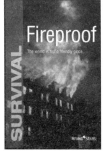